Journey to the Heart Waters

Louisa Calio (signature)

Louisa Calio

Journey to the Heart Waters

LEGAS

Library of Congress Cataloging-in-Publication Data

Calio, Louisa, 1947-
 [Poems. Selections]
 Journey to the Heart Waters / Louisa Calio.
   pages cm
 ISBN 978-1-939693-02-0 (pbk.)
 I. Title.
 PS3603.A4389A6 2014
 811'.6--dc23

                              2014036937

Acknowledgements

The publisher is grateful to Arba Sicula for a generous grant that in part made the publication of this book possible.

For information and for orders, write to:

Legas

P.O. Box 149   3 Wood Aster Bay
Mineola, New York   Ottawa, Ontario
11501, USA   K2R 1D3 Canada

                    legaspublishing.com

Dedication

"There's no one more openly irreverent than a lover. He or she jumps up on the scale opposite eternity and claims to balance it. And there is no one more secretly reverent."

Rumi

"Love is the levitation power over the wounds of gravity."

Ann Ree Colton

In memory of my Sicilian Grandparents, Antonino Calio and Luigia Gianno Calio, my mother, Rosa, whose spirit informs much of my journey and Kassau Tsadik, a courageous Eritrean mother.

Very Special thanks to

My many friends and family from Eritrea and Sudan for sharing themselves and the magic of their lands and cultures, most especially my guides, Dawit, Aster, Yohannis, Abdulla, and the entire Medhanie family, especially Professor and author Tesfatsion Medhanie.

To my benefactor, Volney Ashley Fray, who believed in and supported my work over the years.

Many Thanks to:

Professor Gaetano Cipolla, scholar, publisher, and extraordinary guide to Sicily and its culture.

Antonino Provenzano, Award winning Sicilian poet.

Arba Sicula for helping me re-discover and recover my Sicilian heritage.

Dr. Henry Louis Gates, Jr. & Dr. Robert Farris Thompson for their friendship and opening me to the brilliant cultures of Africa.

Lucia Chiavola Birnbaum whose work on the Black Madonnas of Sicily and the world and their ties to mother Africa is unrivaled.

Photos may not be reproduced without the author's permission.

Acknowledgements:

"Sky Openings: Khartoum", page 16, first appeared in **The New Voices**, (Trinidad & Tobago) Vol. X No. 20, July Issue 1982 Edited by Anson Gonzalez and won The Taliesin Prize for Poetry.

A version of "Bhari" pp. 17-18, 23 won First Prize in the IV Concorso Di Poesia Internationale Messina Citta D'Arte, Sicily, November 30, 2013. This poem will appear in Journal of Italian Americana, Summer Issue 2015, edited by Michael Palma.

"Perhaps the Desert Will Speak", page 20, was first published in **Philadelphia Poets 2011, Volume 17—Spring 2011 issue,** edited by Rosemary Petracca Cappello.

"Black Madonnas", pp. 24-25, was published in **Gradiva**, an International Journal of Poetry, Vol. #30 Fall issue 2006 edited by Luigi Fontanella.

"Mystery of the Sexes", pp. 33, was first published under the title "Cradling through Time" in the collection: **IN THE EYE OF BALANCE** (New York: Paradiso Press, 1978) by Louisa Calio.

"Dance of Gold", page 51, was first published in **Philadelphia Poets 2011, Volume 17—Spring 2011 issue** edited by Rosemary Petracca Cappello.

"Sacred Dancer", page 59, was published in **Salome**, a literary and dance magazine, Vol. 30-31 Chicago, Ill. in 1983, and in a self published chapbook by Louisa Calio 1983 entitled **Sacred Dancer** as well as part of a performance piece with Cheri Miller & the Tapestry Dancers.

"Desert elegance turned to Dust", page 65, and "Today I Walk with a Soldier", pp. 66-67, first appeared in "Premonitions of Iraq: War, Women and Healing" a look at Somalia in Dr. Lina Unali's book, **Somali Queen Somali King,** and poems of Eritrea by Louisa Calio in **Italian Americans and the Arts & Culture** edited by Mary Jo Bona, Dawn Esposito and Anthony Julian Tamburri Selected essays for American Italian Historical Assoc. Vol. # 36, 2005.

"Khartoum Telatta" pp. 68-70 appeared under the title "Eritrea, My Ithaca" in **Feile Festa vol.1 spring issue** 2006, edited by Frank Polizzi, and won the Barbara Jones Prize for Poetry awarded by **The New Voices**, Trinidad & Tobago in 1984 and later appeared with an essay in 2008, entitled *In Search of a Larger Truth: Eritrea, My Ithaca" by* Louisa Calio in an anthology entitled: *Birthed from Scorched Hearts: Women Respond to War,* edited by MariJo Moore. **Publisher**: Fulcrum Publishing, Golden, Colorado 80403 in 2008. ISBN: 978-1-55591-665-7

All photos copyrighted by Louisa Calio.

Table of Contents

Prologue 9

Arrival 12

Sky Openings 16

Bhari 17

Black Madonnas 24

Flashback USA '76 26

Love in Separation 41

London 49

Amarat a Khartoum Suburb 53

Sufis at Omdurman 56

Moonfight/ White Nile 60

Desert Elegance Turns to Dust 65

Today I Walk with a Soldier 66

Khartoum Telatta, Refugee Camp 68

Lifting the Veils 71

Lover of the Gentle Heart 73

Departure: Beside the Blue Nile 75

Plate I - *The Blue Nile Ferry* 19
Plate II - *The Sahara near Amarat.* 19
Plate III - *Sufi (whirling dervish) in Lepard Skins at (Omdurman)* 58
Plate IV - *Women at a graveyard watching near Omdurman* 58

Louisa Calio in a Zuria, traditional Eritrean dress 1978

My Paternal Aunt, Mariann Calio-Nappi (right) born in Palermo
With her cousin Suzette (left) in Tripoli 1929

Prologue

Khartoum, the capital of Sudan, is located in the predominantly Moslem north of this East African nation. It is the seat of the two Niles and the ancient Nubian culture, which is now considered to predate Egyptian culture. A multicultural crossroads for thousands of years, it most recently was home to millions of refugees from neighboring nations. Eritrea, a former Italian colony (1890-1941) and a British colony under its caretaker government (1941-1950), was annexed to Ethiopia at the end of World War II to exploit its strategic location on the Red Sea. For over thirty years, Eritrea fought a war of independence. In the late 1970's many Eritrean refugees were forced to flee as a result of the escalation of bombings in this primarily agrarian country. One of the first nations to receive them was Sudan.

In WONDERS OF THE AFRICAN WORLD, Henry Louis Gates, Jr. writes, "Nubia today denotes not just the geographical region of northern Sudan and Southern Egypt. It has come to stand for all that has been lost or stolen from the historical record of Blacks" ... and as Sicilian American scholar/author Lucia Chiavola Birnbaum writes, all those others, including women, Sicilians, southern Italians and other non-dominant groups. Chiavola-Birnbaum concludes and Gates writes, "until the West and the rest of us know Africa, we can never know ourselves."

When one is awakened by a soul call, we may find ourselves going to faraway places, and in my case, making a journey to Sudan in 1978. At the time, I had no idea my Sicilian Aunt, Mariann Calio, had made a similar journey to Africa at about the same age (28 years old) or how close Sicily was to Africa historically, as well as geographically. My father's sister went to visit her Cousin Suzette and the part of our family who lived in Libya, then called Tripoli in 1929. They had worked as translators for the Italian government and also for the Bank of Sicily in Libya. I learned many Sicilians were also sent to Eritrea in the late 1870's as cheap labor after Italian Unification. These laborers would help develop the railways of Eritrea and eventually build Asmara, its famed capital, which looks like an Italian city. Palermo has a boulevard named for Asmara.

"I had come to the place of the long view of history", where one seeks to better know her own soul and the causes of her story. I was immediately made more aware of my feminine struggle and its sources on arrival in Khartoum. The sense that women are not seen as fully human, becomes quite palpable in a place where women were chaperoned wherever they went and would later be forced back into being covered and made invisible. It was equally clear that women were bringing in the new. Many were highly educated and free by the mid-70's. Most wore wraps and scarves only as decoration, but this was to change. There

was so strong a feeling of the feminine rising wherever I went, the growing voice of women, that it may have awakened the fear behind the recent return to fundamentalism in Sudan.

__Journey to the Heart Waters__ is divided into three sections: Part1, Poems of The Arrival: Khartoum 1978 when I am almost barred from entering. Part 2, the memory of what inspired the journey, and Part 3, the actual journey which involved stopping in London where I was guided and prepared for the trip by three women. The experiences in Sudan would open me to a higher vision, beyond the confinements of ordinary time and limiting duality. Each poem exists within this narrative context. The call to East Africa began unconsciously in my youth with childhood images of the great eye of Horus and dreams of the desert. The trip was inspired by matters of heart, a profound alchemical passion would evoke what Jung refers to as matters of the soul and the seeming impossible splits that come with conflicting opposites. With love, also came loss and separation, introspection and finally clear guidance and understanding. In Sudan, prompted by these highly charged environs: the desert, the two Niles, and the cultures of Nubia and Eritrea, I would recognize the archetypal nature of my experience, as well as the more personal to finally realize a larger understanding of who I really am. Each experience happened in real time. I met my greatest fears and longings and was given an opportunity to know first hand some of my own family's story, especially the story tied to Sicily, the land of my paternal ancestors.

I had come to re-meet an Eritrean from Asmara that I had known in America. As an Italian /American I felt a deep connection to Eritrea, a former Italian colony. I had a profound empathy for the trauma of culture loss, and the Diaspora of the Eritrean people. This put me in closer touch with what my ancestors had experienced. The similarities we shared from our common exposure to Italian culture drew us together in inexplicable ways. The trip was generations in the making. Many Sicilians who were sent to Eritrea by the monarchy were masons. My friend's father learned masonry and construction from them as well as the Italian language. My beloved friend and I were also part of the 60's generation and shared similar ideals. Eritrea mirrored a part of my lost heritage that was grounded in peasant-feudal traditions, only partially erased by the American experience and the 60's revolution.

Going to Sudan brought me face to face with many families seeking a better life, an escape from refugee camps, from the horrors of war, the pain of separation and the confusion of cultural clashes which I carried in my own DNA. This book is a poetic expression of these experiences.

WAR AND A WOMAN

War and a woman I sing.
A country
Needs a woman
to find peace.

Only a woman
can sacrifice enough
to overcome fear,
win the fight
and still keep peace in sight….

By Dr. Reesom Haile, Poet laureate of Eritrea
Translation from the original Tigrinya
by Dr. Ghirmai Negash and Charles Cantalupo

Ova Signora

When the Italians occupied Asmara
We saved a few chickens
In the old district four.
They got fat on the cheap barley,
So we weren't totally poor.
We sold their eggs
White as fine plaster:
"Ova, Signora. Ova, Signora,"
Till our throats were sore.
Thanks to those chickens we survived
While General Baldisera, fortified for war,
Ate omelets.

By Dr. Reesom Haile , Poet laureate of Eritrea
Translation from Tigrinya by Charles Cantalupo and
Dr. Ghirmai Negash

Arrival - Khartoum Airport (January 1978)

(For the new to be born, the old must be transformed)

When the plane lands
I notice for the first time
aside from the stewardesses
I am the only woman on board.

A pair of dark eyes
embedded in a sea of white fire
watch me from the distance
spelling some of the darkness yet to come.

I feel some genetic code
stir deep within my bones
as I prepare to witness woman in all her stages
from covered face to modern lady.

Despite a change of dress
I still harbor the same old fears
when customs and immigration
confiscate
my courage and my passport
at 2 a.m. Khartoum time.

An official asks me only one question:
"Are You traveling *alone?"*
"Well no, not exactly ... my friends are here ...
out there.
You'll not keep me, where?
Not in this desert-ed airport!"

I center
I will enter...
I tell myself
but dare not gaze too long into those eyes
each protruding vein and blood vessel
a road map of judgment and condemnation
of a woman's freedom
as well as a reminder
that only the laws that lifted the veils of women
had changed,
and not the hearts of the men who made them.

He holds a mirror to my Soul terrors
deep subconscious fears
that wait in ambush
to assail me with the laws of my forefathers
codes that forbade and condemned such acts of audacity.

He digs his heels in.
"No. You will not enter
Your visa is invalid," he lied.

Unconscious fears take me
back to age old warnings
mothers and grandmothers
imparted
about the danger and vulnerability
of a woman traveling alone.

For a moment I try to comprehend
how I may have offended him
with my mere presence.
Does he fear my tender hooks of openness
or the warnings of his forefathers?
Am I the Christian infidel, a temptress
or do I represent a more core terror,
or the sister he could have righteously murdered
for breaking the rules of tradition and law?

Such thoughts do not serve me here
could destroy me now
I tell myself
as doubts continue to swamp me.
Wasn't I called?
Did I read the signs correctly?
I wonder, while he toys with my passport.

His hateful stare intensifies
I feel my courage about to falter...
when that mysterious force
the one that opens doors
enters
in the form of a friend
Abdulla
whose name in Arabic means "God's messenger."

Miraculously, he appears with my Beloved
and I listen while three men
argue my fate in Arabic,
a language I do not comprehend.

I tell myself only one thought
I will get through.

Finally those eyes, once filled with hate
soften to glazed indifference,
and the stamp that opens borders
is placed inside my small blue book.

Open Sesame
I've arrived!

Sky Openings

The night was totally still
empty of any artificial light or sound
as it rarely is in industrial countries
and although you complain
of these troublesome blackouts
the poor electrical connections in Khartoum
for me, so burdened with progress and stress
This was a reprieve--
the sky so close and black except for punctuating stars
I could nearly touch the diamonds
while you walk weighted beside me
an ancestral figure
head filled with thoughts of war, bent you were
with only your eyes touching the heavens.

You said, you didn't want the law or politics anymore-
what then would be next?
We wondered
when the sky brought its unspoken reply.
For once, we didn't drop to the earthly plight
For once we felt -- the space--
                    interplanetary, stellar potential
the end of the Piscean Age
Pressing us to new life!

Bhari- the meeting place of the Blue and White Niles

I stand beside the ancient waters
Nile waters
in the old kingdoms of Nubia, Auxum and Kush
an American woman artist
wandering
in distant regions far from my home.

Why do I roam?
Is it only to seek a lover from another culture
or is there a greater mystery at work
a modern day miracle play
a tribal genesis I am to follow
a labyrinth-like route to my ancient,
ancestral roots?

Wasn't as easy as was thought
to transform in one brush stroke
an Italian to an American.
I had to return to the deeper roots of origin
before Rome or Greece.

I have come to the place of the long view of history
a well crossed route, the Sahara
witness to many civilizations
comings and goings
a twilight land where edges blur
into vast sacred emptiness.

Land helps give shape to us.
A desert cannot be owned or possessed
in this respect, she is closest to our essence.

There are many unanswered questions
in the north of Sudan, a desert land
cut by two lines,
>One blue and tame
>>One white and wild

Cool are the waters of the two Niles
blending to one
as two lovers might.

I ask my inner Nile to yield some message
while I look upon her counterpart
Wise, old Mother, with the shift in light
you look black and white
the polarities of life:
day/night, left/right, male/female
an old dyadic tug.

Is this why you've pulled me to your side
or do you carry me from some other time
to learn an even greater lesson?

In my youth I dreamed you
in childhood, fantasized myself by your side
an Egyptian priestess
dancing desert lady, dancing by a wild-fire
while a tall, thin, olive skinned man looked on
and a tribal people, Bedouin like
came from across the dunes
to sweep us up
on wild horses.

From where did this dream come
river of two and of one?

I ask my inner Nile to yield some message
While I look upon her counterpart
Wise old mother,
With the shift of light you look
black and white
the polarities of life:
day night, left right, male female
an old dyadic tug.

Louisa Calio
A Journey to the Heart Waters

Plates I and II

Perhaps the desert will speak.
    Vast expanse a desert's elegance
                flat- endless- horizon
calling for a sea to balance
she's a Biblical landscape
confirmed
by the tall Sudanese
walking angels in long, white, billowing jelabias
traditional dress that makes sharp contrast
with three Yemeni women passing
in black dress, black mask and black veil.

Eerily, they stop to stoop
into a huge mound of charcoal—
fuel for tomorrow's food.
I wonder how they see the world
through their dark portable prisons
grid work screens that chop their vision
into tiny checker board pieces?
Are they young, old or middle aged?
What shape their eyes, their lips, full or thin?
What color and texture their hair, skin?

Their absence makes such a notable presence
Does anonymity have its gifts and pleasures?
I wonder as I walk
the only woman in pants across a desert land.

Am I equally invisible
unripe, green American
infidel, trespasser to their ancient land?

Sufi men in colorful beaded caps
drumming and chanting by the road side
seem oblivious to my passing.

Only begging leper women
whose uncovered hands
look burned and charred
reach out to me with tolerance.

Ten sparsely clad Dinka men
Appear like Long Shadows
on the horizon.

Emaciated Ebony Giants from Juba
foreheads lined by three thick rows
of initiation scars
wearily pass us
on their way back from the day's labor.

Driven from their once fertile homelands
by war and hunger
they work like slaves in the north for the Arabs
under the desert's scorching sun.

At the University
we meet more westernized men and women.
Some wear colorful sheer pastel veils
tossed casually like scarves
while others wear no veils at all.
Some of the men don the traditional white turban
and gown, but most wear British or American suits.
A few still have on *Caribas*, those once fashionable
khaki bush jackets, a leftist's uniform.

Their garments tell a story of recent history:
a succession of foreign imports
that promised everything,
but left little more than a western appearance
and an arsenal that now supports
a military regime.

We bump into a group of women
demonstrating against the growing popularity
of The *Muslim Brotherhood*, a fundamentalist party
that will return Sudan to *Sharia*, Islamic law—
and send women back into seclusion, *purdah*
to wear b*urka,*
while subjecting all of its people
to the most severe and brutal punishments
even for minor infractions.

Students carry life size placards
a replica of woman under the old law.
She appears mummified,
not a glimpse of human flesh
under endless wraps of white cotton gauze
hands are covered with black gloves
feet enclosed in thick, black leather shoes
baby coffins.
Though most grotesque of all
was the pair of reflective, mirrored goggles she wore
to keep her eyes hidden.
A space alien would appear more human and friendly.

Traveling the desert's ponderous, pale-brown void
dotted with camels, Bedouins
dunes, dates and palms
cypress trees and Nubian Pyramids,
I am taken past the world of small, man- made laws
into a Natural Order.

Cellular memories reawaken.

With each passing
undulation
I am reminded
that I too am
a wave form.

Like an archeologist
I've come to examine the shells of my origins:
Pagan-Italian, Egyptian, Judeo-Christian-Coptic
Nubian- Islamic, Maltese-Sicilian, Greek
to better know all of my parts
including those that remain hidden and dark
veiled and repressed
in regions of the deeper psyche
regions that long for illumination.

After all, it was only yesterday
that I lifted my veils of illusion
the pretense of contentment with a secondary life
a passive role, only to discover
that many more veils lie within
remaining to be revealed.

Black Madonnas

In the small villages
      black madonnas
            fly from me like a flock of ravens

from behind thick red-mud walls
when I approach.

Only men are permitted to extend a greeting.

Yet it is you, my hidden feminine
who linger in my thoughts
and hover around after I leave.
I hear your heart beating softly
and imagine we speak a common language
share our laughter and all of our secrets.

I see your essence, no matter how veiled
waiting like a seed to germinate
like the seed I've carried from my ancestors
flowering in its own timing
to burst forth into a song
a song of joy and freedom
and openly claim your unique, individualized
vitally alive- Self,
kept under wraps
or perverted into some distortion, just to survive.

As you try on these new garments
keep what is truly beautiful
your Nubian ways,
the dances you do when you sway
moving your head
from shoulder to shoulder
side to side
harmonizing your heart with your mind
and keeping the One law always
.... The law of Love.
It alone gives us the power to re-imagine ourselves.

So far we've seen only the surface
of your depths
superficial outer expressions
of the feminine.
Like earth, you hold the key
to the mysteries
within your core
untapped potentials
a call for inner exploration
new tools of navigation
offering a greater knowledge of our spirit/bodies
fashioned by the High God/Goddess.

Who makes this visual joke?
Is this heaven or hell
and I the foreign devil?
I wonder as I walk,
the only woman in pants
across a desert land
Still asking the Mother- Nile for answers.

The Call: Flashback USA 1976

Upheaval comes with lightning swiftness
shattering old thought forms
mercilessly.
Transformation
furious as a storm at sea
rapidly brings my marriage
no longer a challenge to its closing.

Two one time friends
part as strangers, near enemies
painful for the mind and beliefs once held tightly.
Yet new energy is released
a freeing begins
as I begin to paint again
after 5 years, the length of a marriage.
What binds me, my feet?
What or who frees me?

I take to walking nights and swimming days
all feels familiar and yet strange.
I wear black and white often
and visions of fire fill my eyes
but I am unafraid.
I paint and write in journals daily
a new fluidity fills my life.

It seems a time when the unconscious mind
aroused
floods me with its mass of imagery
ancestral memories-
perhaps a Soul's journey
reaching both ahead and back through time
to some inevitable test.

I have heard it said,
such times also give rise
to Greater Intuitions
offering a glimpse at life's larger picture.

And From the Sea of Divine Love
magnificent landscapes come daily
in colors vibrating with energy.
I paint these scenes in rich, thick oils
guided solely by my dreams
in which an old man appears.
He was from another rough, dry terrain
a desert land
and whispered to me nightly,
in a language I could never recall by morning.

This lasted many weeks.
Was he a dream guide
the old man from ancient times?
I asked, never receiving an answer.

With Her arrival all questions cease.
She was the most supremely feminine feeling

From the coolest corner
of the darkest space
at the longest river
of an unseen place,
She
lies in wait,
a force
a feminine force,
Pearl, in the eyes of the world
vulva eyes, lotus eyes,
black-purple slits -that always smile.

Through HER
I was able to abandon everything
and simply sit.

After hours of meditation
I began to write again
words, poems, verses of my soul
which said: I am pure, nurturing, desired
the mothering called for and received.
I am neither of man, nor of woman
but of both.
I am the lover you await
and who awaits you.
Do not be afraid!
I am the Compassionate One
calling to all her luminous beings
go forth and do my bidding.

Feelings so wondrous gripped and ravished me
I felt like a helpless child
in the clutches of what gave new expression
to her name - *Mother*.

That was when He appeared
The familiar looking stranger
who stopped to talk
on one of my midnight walks.

He was the Beloved
of all my paintings come to life.
Attraction to the exotic
materialized.
Krishna, the adored one
and warrior combined;
so much like the man of my childhood fancies
I was irresistibly drawn in-
to a sea of desire.

He too was aware of the pull
having been prepared
by many months of dryness
nothing but study, hours of political worry
and a type of loneliness
only a foreigner knows.

He was a continuation of unfinished conversations
at my Grandfather's table when I was a child
and took in many meals of political debate
and hopes for the underprivileged.

He was my haunting inner questions:
dare I create and make art, while others still suffer?
Where does individuality begin
and responsibility end?

He was Eritrean, from a land
my ancestors invaded
spoke the Italian language, which I could not
offered me bread and roses
delicious conversations
and dinners of heart.

I couldn't have invented this perfect jigsaw-puzzle
fit of matching pieces:
pagan-Christian, colonized-free-spirit,
anti-establishment- conservative-radical,
fearful of strangers, daring- lover.

I was the food that he missed at his father's table
where many an Italian colonial had been
the uninvited guest,
who took ancestral lands
sent his grandfather to fight in Tripoli
taught his father masonry and his mother to cook
a most savory, peppery tomato sauce with *zighini*.

We had joked that it was probably
our grandfathers' ghosts
who had prearranged this meeting
but in truth, I sensed
it was his mother's prayers to Miriam
that brought him to me.

We were born of those waves of invasions
that left lingering marks and scarifications
tell tale signs and woundings
I had learned to read early
on my grandfather's lap.
When he had spoken of the poor
disowned, disenfranchised and oppressed,
a fiery glow would come over him
filling his throat and chest
with a thunderous cry
a voice that shook me all over.
Emotions, erupting like hot lava
cultivated new ground
with a longing
for power
authentic power, a gentler power
he would never live to see bear fruit,
a longing that had cut off his joy at the feet.

Railing against his enemies
who could never hear him
the heartless and the greedy
who had shamed him when they sent him
to the back door for work,
dared imply he could be a fascist,
led me to witness a Soul ache so great
beyond the loss of Italy
or disappointments in America
an ache so deep and fathomless
only future generations
could hope to heal and restore.

There is a legendary magic
in the reconciliation of opposites
meeting of black and white
of former ancestral enemies
colonizer and colonized
of water and fire.

It seemed kind Mother Nature
had yielded some of her very best stuff.
Love, meetings daily
guided by no more than the sun.
I was woman, body and soul
living all of her roles:
healer, mistress, mothering one,
inspired energizer,
deep from within the wellspring
I had come
cradling
some of life's most powerful energies.

What more is there than this?
Love is bliss!
Nothing more, nothing less
than the essence of the mysteries.

Mystery of the Sexes

> "If anything is sacred, the human body is."
> Walt Whitman

Coming from separate worlds
we crawl inside under cover
black, black velvet night.
Freed from the skins that cannot feel
we hold on tight
touching the layers
we're born with.

Twins in the womb of the world
boy-girl, girl-boy, rolling, rolling
switching as we wish
in the cradle you and I rock
face to face, back to back, side to side
In our minutes of eternity
I understand the sacredness of unity.

Moisture surrounds, mists, clouds, waters
moving in rhythm
uncoiling the spirals inside
a soft shell I,
echoing the sea
wet copper wires.

I change the time, you change the time
we make new rhythms, unheard of times
fearless inventions, tempos, patterns, times.
I study you more intensely
than any subject of my life.
I learn
what frees you, soothes you
brings you to thunderous cries
trans-fers to my insides
in thun-der time.
You learn
the more delicate motions
take me to my highest cries
Mountains rise, rise
I am a shriek; I am the sky.

Mountains, streams, seas
remnants of origins
primal screams,
freed of the cerebral web
we cradle the cradle of civilizations,
our heads forget
allowing our insides to remember.
Yes, I can come again.

He had awakened "The Current"

Wet and luscious as a snake it comes
to make your body whole
the million- million thoughts
dissipate,
and a calm current flows at a steady rate.
Nature,
lush and abounding as the five scents of Eve
passes through you and through me.
desert sands, salt seas
even we,
passing.

Never had my spirit-body
known such an ecstasy
as in those forty nights and days of loving,
or a peace so profound and empowering
I could feel my heart trembling.

From where does this love come
that goes through my heart like electric-shock
that illumines you and illumines me?

From deep, deep, deep
it comes
Deep as where the ancestors sleep
my Beloved said to me.

Perhaps, this was too great an ecstasy
and like the desert
that calls for a sea to balance
this love by necessity
called for its equal opposite, magnetic polarity.

Had our parting
come as a natural tendency,
the gradual falling off of intensity
a seeping boredom between two lovers
it may not have called for
both the drowning and burning of this soul,
but this soul seemed destined
for life's harder lessons.

Intoxicated with love,
I refused to see what was before me.

His demeanor was cloudy.
Clarity, gave way to a strange perplexity
expressed by a deep furrow in his brow.
He was noticeably
much less in the here and now
frequently observing the passing of time.
An energy that once spread throughout his body
seemed to be clogged in the region of the head
a head full of reasons
that argued against
the dangers of passion.

Feelings in fragment
frightened him.
He wondered,
how could love fit in a life already so split
complicated with strife,
factionalized as his country by warring parts:
Marxist, Moslem, Christian, old world and new
Is he to be torn by an American too!
While these thoughts grew in power
I foolishly created a work of art
as a living testimony to matters of the heart.
Ignorantly, I unveiled

A Sacred Painting:

Wearing robes of regal white
on a throne carved and shaped by golden light
he sat amid ancient symbols.
His left arm reached skyward
like the magician's in the Tarot
to his side stood the old man, my dream guide
father time with a long staff in hand
I kneeled to his right, unclothed
save for a glow of violet light
created by a distant fire,
His hand touching and anointing
my face - an ecstatic saint's.

It was not only that this love was blind
though it was by its very nature
a blinding light
or that it was tied to no other parts of our lives
that made it such a grave danger,
but dealing so often in a world of imagery,
I had forgotten the true sources of nourishment
and began to believe
that He held the keys to my life's destiny.

With his withdrawal went the sun
as well as the moon's light.
Bridled by fear and desire
I became a mad woman
stalking him by night,
and only by night did he let me in
denying me in daylight's presence.

I tried to be contented with this arrangement
but attachment had set its claws in
like a falcon's.
Where once love had been,
was now only a grasping.
The tighter I held
the greater was his resistance.
He literally ran from one land to another
flying to Sudan in aid of an ailing brother
and the many Eritrean refugees in need.

So great was my hunger
so great the loss
a tunnel of sorrow swallowed me
down
      down
            down
to the veritable origins of grief,
a grief of so great an intensity,
it equaled love's ecstasy.

Darkness devoured
layering black upon black,
making a cloak of my grimness
as heavy as death.
Pressure bearing down
paralyzed my panic
with its heavy blows.

Each night I was awakened
by profuse sweats
taunted by the images of darkness
bloodletting, a slow, thick oozing
preceded a picture of a gaping wound
in my chest,
stacks of torn, mutilated human flesh,
broken bones and corpses piled high,
all oddly fitting.

I could no longer separate day from night
All life's suffering seemed to congeal
at first into a hard, black spot
then to a searing white hot knot
burning at the very center of my heart.

I had merged into a vast sea
of human sorrowing
- where once had been the sea of love.

It could have been no worse for St. Sebastian
whose flesh was pierced by scores of arrows.
I imagined those arrows
gathering to one
that ripped, seared
and pierced my being
tearing it into pieces.

Burrowing in
I risked everything and surrendered to the dark.

Then a quiet came
- a stillness so profound
it hushed all of my pain
and turned grief into peace
refilling my life's container.

Emerging from the darkness
the figure of a woman,
bare breasted goddess
shimmering in mermaid greens and aquamarines
knee-deep in sea-foam,
she emerged from crystal waters
and touched me with her ancient sources,
renewing, reviving and restoring
my life forces.

Love in Separation: USA The Same Winter

Another leap in consciousness:
Love from within
need never be returned or lost.

Love is its own completion
its own reward
and knows no boundaries.

This was my inner knowing
and not mere thinking.
I sent this love to many people
and to Him
now living in the desert
helping with waves of refugees
from his land, a bordering nation
at war.

As great as the love I felt for him
was his love and grief for his country.
Through this understanding
oneness was born to us again.

The pen became my paintbrush
as I richly expressed my love and solemn plea
to take our lives
beyond the confines of human history.
I pledged to write daily
sending only my better efforts.

We began a dialectic:
a reflection of our opposing
yet connecting views.

Beloved,

Your people do a Snake dance.
It echoes the great dance
that goes on and on endlessly.
It is the dance of pure formless energy
the dance of the world
and we are its two currents
man and woman
whose union will bring about
the tide of change
we seek
a new wave we can ride together
to earth's re-centering
humanity's rebirthing
returning us all to more natural rhythms.

Only this will lead to a healing
and the redistribution
of wealth of which you speak.

Friend,

Thank you for your concerns.
I am, however, very busy, too busy to write.
There is so much work to be done.
I can't believe how many of my people are dying.
I am caught. I must do my part,
but what is my part
when there are so many in need?
You are lucky.
Your land is rich,
filled with momentary prosperity,
developed at the expense of the less privileged,
but you had no control over this.
Stay away from this gloom.
I am sick with sorrow.
My people from Hazaga were bombed.

Beloved,

I long to send you words to heal by
and thoughts to soothe you with
Consider the deeper causes of things.
Hard as it may be
try not to be guided solely by your surroundings.
They may have grave effect,
and still not reflect the whole truth,
segments rarely do.

Am I here to remind you
of other realities and possibilities?
Ask why you feel you must bear
your heritage like a cross?
Could this be the old Coptic forces
guilt and sacrifice at work?

Will your pain and misery benefit your land,
or is it your light and love that offer service?
Please, preserve it!

You often speak of the responsibilities of the rich and powerful;
yet, are they less ignorant?
Is it really about changing ideologies
or the unbending of our beliefs
we need change?
Let's follow the river's curves and bends,
she ever resurfaces again.

Beloved,

I've longed for you so many nights
feeling the void inside.
Don't be afraid to enter silence,
a woman's chamber.
There is great relief here.

We are the galaxies in miniature.
Didn't my moon-love give birth to a sun
from mountains of pressure and sorrow
crushing me to a seed again
making me as hard as a gem?

Arise, oh my shining one,
my Diamond Gem
ever I will be
Your Ruby-Red.

Friend,

Your words are nice, kind and sweet,
but you are much too idealistic
and I am from a doomed history.

Forget me and marry a nice American.
My life, like my country's, is war torn.
How can I dream of rebirth or a new earth?
I see only the displaced, maimed and hungry.

Beloved,

Can words heal? Do songs soothe?
Do I make love to you through a poem?
It's much easier to see the world's flaws
and make them separate from our own.

Can they be?
Which is easier to act upon?

>**Violet & indigo are we**
>the double edge of life
>born of Compassion, not of strife.
>Joy is our true heritage, not grief!

We, like the universe, are expanding
seeded by the stars.
I have opened my eyes
and seen worlds
come from between my thighs!
Inspired, I fly to you.

I will arrive late Khartoum time.

After long silence, a Telegram:
Under No Circumstances
are you to come to Sudan.
It is far too dangerous.
I repeat, do not come.
I will not receive you!

Sharp was the sting of those words.
His inner whip having driven him
for being among the living
now struck out at me.

I was not yet strong
in my newly acquired vision.
The words reopened old wounds.
Would I fall again?

I chanted and chattered
to distract myself
as my fears gathered.

Hanging on to the little lights
I was afraid she'd be back
the woman dressed in black
ravenous, afire,
nearly always on the rack.

Had not some higher forces
already been set into motion
his message could have ended
this pilgrim's progress
right there and then.

Despite my inner fears and terror
I remained committed
to follow this heartline
to the end.
If only I knew how
if only I knew when
to make my next move.

Let there be a sign
I implored.
I thought of the black Madonna of Sicily
and all fabled lore
that promised to aid
one on a quest.
I prayed and did not rest.

Perhaps my plea
had sent a radiation
      a vibration so strong and empowering
            it reached the outer edges~ of eternity
to the ocean of infinity
where all things are born.

For after my call came
not one,
but THREE startling messages
to answer all my questions:

A
Pyramid of Energy

Appearing in a dream
beauty in blue, veiled woman, Madonna
or queen rising on a radiant, crescent moon
beckoned me to follow
through space and time
to the banks of an ancient beautiful river
two rivers,
the Nubian Niles!

The second came in the form of a letter
written by our friend
"God's messenger"
which read
"I will meet you upon arrival.
Disregard any prior message."
Your friend
Abdu

Three, a trinity, magical number
                    triple, triangular energy
                                        brought into manifestation

a final message
from an English school friend
who invited me to stay with her in London
while enroute to Khartoum.

And I was gone.

The Journey: London (in transit)

I was met
not by one
but THREE English friends.
Three women I had known at college
as artists
now called themselves witches.
Strange profession!

In London, they explained
my aura was sullied.
They could obviously see
something was worrying me.
A bluish-gray haze
lay over my head
giving away my current state.

Closing their eyes, arms raised high
each helped create
a pyramidal shape
that lovingly radiated warmth
from their hands
to the crown of my head.
I was soon giddy and light, a sheer delight.
Was this a healing?

Later in the evening we played music
Indian drums lifted my remaining weights.

And I was taught a "Dance of Silver"

Pure grace
long, lithe and lean movements
sparkling flecks of dancing lights
with silvery specks
green enchanted forests,
fairy dust, gnomes and elves
and other Celtic fancies sprung to mind
while we danced
what felt an old Druid rite
came back to life.

Before I'm to go, I'm told
I must also learn
the "Dance of Gold"
three lovely witches agree over tea.

Dance of gold
pure horizontals—
the epitome of an immovable, pressing destiny
is danced to meet a target, achieve a goal.

Left arm drawn like a bow
right, straight as an arrow,
pointed ahead.
As power concentrated
this dance looked red
although, a golden glow showed
around the slow deliberate steps
of all the participants.

Warned to use it sparingly
because of its power
it can become diffuse from over-use
I am told
it will evoke the Warrior's Soul
and that the warrior
made up one half of my soul.

Misty-eyed and mystified
I was ready to leave
when I am given one last gift
a reading
from a book whose name
had to remain secret.

"Do not be afraid.
You are not alone.
There are many guides to help.
You do the great work,
the work of your time.
Just listen, watch,
and follow the signs.

Reach into your center
unify your heart with your mind
you will achieve your goal.
Many who do this work become clouded
by their culture and surroundings.
Stay clear and be forewarned
do not let these outward signs deter you.
Stick to the light."

Mumbo Jumbo said my head
while yet another sign was made manifest.
At a bookshop at Heathrow,
a copy of *The Divine Horsemen* by Maya Deren
seemed to leap at me from the shelf.
With no more time for thought
I bought it and boarded.

Amarat- a Khartoum suburb

Magical moments offering
fleeting glimpses of our potential
open new doors
briefly filling us with light
and just as swiftly
shut down tight
under the pressures of ordinary life.

Man of Iron,
after my arrival
you returned to your grave and embedded ways
Willed to show me
in your every pose
I should have obeyed
I should have stayed
in my place
at home in America
where I belonged.

So too could I see
the pressure he remained under
while he took on the plight
of his countryman in flight,
many had asked for advice, aid or shelter.

Refugees filled his life and his house
as well as many relations, uncles, cousins,
and soldiers, young and old in need
of temporary lodging
or help in adapting to a foreign land.

I lived in two deserts
one, blazing hot
one, cold as ice.
I was the stranger
like your refugees
seeking a kind, familiar face,
a gesture I could recognize
someone who speaks my language.

I often thought of my immigrant grandparents,
Could I have been as brave as they
during their first days in America
with no way back home?

Were they as lonely as I
in the desert of my choosing?

I read Maya most days
and when I can't sleep nights.
Books have often come to my aid
when people have failed to.
This book becomes key to my journey.

Another woman artist on a quest
leaves for Haiti from the US
to film dance
and finds herself absorbed
in the experience of Voudoun-
a religion of ecstatic communion.

Why does anyone journey
to strange shores and deserts?
I think of history, the ancient mysteries
to find the true source of Self
face one's demons and perhaps return the wiser.

Communicating with higher forces,
call them what you will
invisibles, angels, saints
guides or archetypes,
these higher energies
are known to intervene
in human destiny
when implored.

I decide to try and reach them
Haitian style
seeking the aid of Erzulie, Queen of Hearts
Empress of the Tarot cards.
I ask that she create abundance for me
make it rain in the desert.

Instinctively, I know it will take more
than just words to move this source of power.
With all of my concentration
I mentally paint her
focusing my complete attention
upon her every detail.
Each line of loveliness
from face to form
I give shape to
and build an altar for her sake
noting
with her growing presence
came the knowledge
that it was my own doubts and fears
that had kept him from me.

Iron was tempering...

Sufis at Omdurman

Our Sudanese friend invited us to visit
one of the oldest parts of the city
 Omdurman
        at dusk
                is all the East ever was
domed-shaped mosques and minarets
rising pointed peaks of gold
peering through a fine red dust
light violet hours of quietude
still and silent beings
moving across an ocean of infinity:
the Sahara
squared by rows of red-mud huts.

Near to a graveyard
behind the oldest mosque,
we joined a group gathering for an ancient rite.
Men dressed in a wide array of clothing,
tattered and torn patch work quilts and rags,
leopard skins and jelabias
formed a circle around a central pole
to begin the ancient Sufi dance
in a counterclockwise motion
Dervishes whirled to the sounding of drums
Chanting: Allah, Al-lah, Al-lah
into the stars at twilight.

Of course, I hadn't noticed at first
this was another version of the Haitian rites
Sufi style!

Living archetypes paraded before me
when I stepped inside the circle
fearful I'd be entranced
by the Sufis gripping chants.

I recognized Llegba dressed in white
Keeper of the Gates
the one who lets us pass over to the other side
in order to communicate.

A man in leopard skins, spear in hand
leapt high above the crowd
pure athletic prowess
Force-Power-The Dance of Gold!
He must be Ogun, the warrior's soul.

Since women were not permitted to participate
I never expected to see Erzulie
make her grand entrance
when, before my eyes
the oldest man transformed,
his every gesture
the sweetest expression
of the divine feminine.

Plates III and IV

Sacred Dancer

He does not smile
this is a sacred dance
s/he is laughing
as s/he sways deep in the hips
offering her breasts, her lips
throws back her head boldly
lets it move slowly
shoulder to shoulder
side to side
down to her knees s/he slides
dancing
s/he shows us the secret child.

Always we are dancing
Whirling the world
We are the rainbow colors in twirl.
Make as the earth
make as the sun,
the motion of ocean
the hum.

After the night at Omdurman
things between us changed for the better.
My Beloved and I
were in sheer delight and total contentment
until the night of the full moon in Aries
at the close of March.

Moonlight, Moonfight/ Party by the White Nile

Back to back
on two full moon nights
we met the two extremes inside.

The red dust of the Sahara was rising
thick clouds masked nearly everything en route,
save the sound of wild dogs
that plagued the town.
How had I failed to heed these signs
when we stepped inside a private party
some Sudanese friends had prearranged?

In a courtyard surrounded by high walls
several African men and mostly foreign women
sat listening to music, dining, and drinking beer and wine
outdoors under the stars.

I wondered when the remaining
Sudanese women would join in,
until I remembered the tradition
that kept them hidden.

It wasn't long before all the men
had drifted to one side, talking politics
and the women remained behind
talking about them.

Out of the corner of my eye
I glimpsed a woman in blue veil
with hair the color of fire.
Was she beige, brown or white?
I could barely see in the light
as she beckoned me follow,
and follow I did
down serpentine corridors
that led me far into
the women's quarters
to what was apparently a very large kitchen.
There Sudanese women of varied ages
sat before a television or off to one side
praying or playing among their many children.

But who was *She,*
this mysterious red-haired woman?
An American from Hawaii she informed me
who had met and married her Sudanese husband
while they attended college in the states.

He had persuaded her to come back
and visit his family and country
a decision she deeply regretted.
Softly and urgently she whispered to me,
"Never marry one of them, no matter what you feel.
You can never belong here. Save yourself!"

She had lived a lonely existence,
five long years in the desert
refusing to learn Arabic, her only act of protest.
I asked why she just didn't leave.
Tears welled her soft green eyes when she spoke
"It would be too terrible a shame for him if I left,
a disgrace in the eyes of family and community
and I would have to leave my children behind.
It's the law."

I felt a deep shiver inside,
as I witnessed the sorrow and pain
of this woman living in twilight,
neither foreign visitor, nor kitchen-wife.
How different these customs
How painful her self-imposed exile.
How she glowed in moonlight.

I cannot put into words precisely what I felt
at the sight of these women, my hidden feminine,
or the common bond we shared
that night in the kitchen.

My Beloved and I left the party in a strange discomfort
mine a feminine resentment
his, the result of political disagreements.

We walked side by side
yet apart
as the fine red dust
became an engulfing fog.

We were pure tension,
pulling together, pulling apart
when he mentions
that it's best we remain apart
just in case one of his countrymen sees us together
and exploits his friendship with an American
in a dust storm in the dark!

Suddenly my remaining composure
newly won detachment and the little wisdom
I had gleaned
fell apart.
His words struck me like a blow
I was wild as the dogs that had gathered near by
and with a voice that was near to a hiss,
replied, "Shall I walk ten feet behind?"

His large eyes transformed
into huge black, burning coals
and yet, I still couldn't resist
courting his demons.
I felt impelled to yell
"And you dare to call yourself Progressive!"
(a favorite term of his and his contemporaries).

Before I could utter another sound
my throat was gripped
by what felt like a pair of invisible hands
preventing what nearly slipped
worse insults than I imagined myself capable of
and the word "Coward" so temptingly near my lips!

I dread the thought of what could have transpired
Surely we both would have been lost
had not my fire subsided
had I not realized
that my passion for him
was no different
than his for his country
my fire no less ravishing.

Angrily, he stormed off into the dense, dark
leaving me alone
to face a pack of wild dogs!
In terror, I prayed, calling on Erzulie, Mother Mary
all the saints and Goddesses to please come to my aid.
Shouting into the bleak night,
I pleaded with him to come back and save me!
Frozen, unable to move
          the dogs began to circle and bark.

Had this been the source of
woman's false composure?
Did we depend on men for protection?
Paralyzed with fear I waited
and finally did hear
his faint footsteps
when he reappeared out of the dark red cloud.

Gathering six stones,
he hurled them
one by one
at the wild dogs that scattered, yelped and cowered.
"They're all bark," he said.
Had I been less afraid
I might have better appreciated
the irony of his remark
and the opaque mirror
offered that night
in the sand and in the dark.

Desert Elegance Turns to Dust
when the Sahara's cruelest weapon
Haboob
a sand storm
descends full blown.

We can do no more than huddle indoors
covering from head to foot
in layers of white muslin cloth
that help prevent our lungs
from sucking in
the fine red stuff.

This same wild night brings a pounding at the door.
My friend approaches cautiously
conscious that such storms
often harbor criminals
who use the dust for cover.

Tonight, five young men appear.
Embracing my beloved are his younger brothers
travelers from Eritrea.
Across a war torn land they came
by camel and Land-Rover,
aided by their 65 year-old mother!

Today I Walk with the Soldier

He, like each of his brothers, is unique.
Although he has been a fighter for seven years
he looks youthful and childlike
and feels more vibrant and alive
than my beloved or me.
Doesn't he worry about dying?

We walk silently side by side.
He stands close and protectively
while we listen attentively to our environ
as though it holds a secret, unspoken tongue.

He questions me, gently
"What do you think of the fighting, my lady?"
But I say nothing as we continue walking
under the desert's burning mid-day sun,
unlike the Sudanese
who wisely remain sheltered indoors.

He takes me for a soda
one of the few drinks available in the desert
he already knows the way
to a small wooden stand
in the middle of nowhere.
I laugh, because the soda makes me more thirsty.

He recalls the cool mountain town he is from
that he was a highlander once
and longs for the cool, crisp, clear mountain air.
I tell him about my visit to the Rockies
with my sister last year.

We speculate, about where he may live next,
whether he'll be able to escape the lowlands he abhors.
He speaks with gratitude for his brother
who has kept their family out of Kassala
and other refugee camps
more like a father, since theirs passed.

He wonders if he will ever see home again.
I peer into his eyes like a crystal gazer
seeing my own ancestral diaspora.

I ask him how he handles all the death and loss
"Acceptance," he responds.
"It's part of our sacrifice
like the one your country made in its revolution.
When a fighter dies,
we make a prayer and bury him
if we can.
We do our best
we live close to each other
we learn to let go."

I think
How unlike me,
as the sun finally drives us indoors.

Khartoum Telatta, a refugee camp

Weeks pass and the young men and I grow closer.
We visit refugee camps regularly,
and on one particularly bright day,
a day when people and objects
appear closer and more luminous,
we meet an old and beautiful Eritrean woman.

In the purple light of dusk we sit
inside a small concrete hovel
sipping the thick sweet coffee she offers.
Still wearing the traditional
pristine, white muslin dress
and veil of her ancestors,
she appears insular
separated from external surroundings.
I watch, as she moves gracefully
despite the confining space
joyfully scooping the dark coffee beans
into a small black iron pan
she holds over on a charcoal flame,
making a fresh pot for each round of servings.
She smiles warmly as I ingest the delicious aromatic brew.
Her hospitality and generosity have remained,
even under these circumstances;
the simple ritual we share binds her to me
and to all those who have stayed compassionate
while living in hell and under fire.

Although we cannot speak a common language,
when it's time to leave, these words come to me
in a deep impress:

"Fix your eyes on a thousand, thousand stars
in the black dome of sky,
stars that do not shine, but spit hell fire.
Look on the sweet earth,
parting, exploding,
earth our fathers worked with sweat.
Look, but don't walk on it;
it may become your gravesite tonight!

See the flowers, rose petals,
only thorns are left.
This is my song today, yes.
Think of those you love dearly,
now think of losing them, multiply this 4 million times
and surely your loss will have touched mine.
My name is Eritrea, South Africa, Somalia, Iraq
my name is America, before and after the European...
I am an Eritrean,
though I was told by your country
I am to be Ethiopian.
I am sure you were not told of that.

The scars of many tears cover my face,
          — my struggle an endless battle cry.
Was my beauty the cause of this
or the buried treasures within
that attracted so many of them:
Italian, Turk, Arab, Greek?
Too many to name
have come and ravished me.
Taking, taking, so much greed!

How I would prefer to speak to you
of our customs and dress.
The netsala women wear covers my head.
The table we set is seated with eight
—we share one plate.
Our land is also shared—divided by lot.
We are many kinds of people and speak many languages.

How I long to tell you of our cool highlands
our capital--Asmara-- as it was...
our desert, touched by the Red Sea
the sea that led Moses to freedom
shall see freedom in me
Red, red now with the blood of my children.

Wars are interminable separations
My children are all refugees or dead.
Who will pay this blood debt?
We are still fighting the wars of possession
my gods, your gods
my land, your land
my race, your race.
We remain locked in the jaws of separation
each regretful act justified by past dreadful deeds
ever recreating the patterning of pain.
We are not yet making unity;
we are not yet making peace.
Each branch of learning remains at war
as we remain caught in contradictions.

Today I will call myself human being.
Will you join me?
All of the colors make one light
why stay in the dark?
The speed of light is very great
Just imagine where we could be!

We each need the same basic things:
a blazing sun, a golden glow around everyone
enough to live, enough to eat, to love.

There seem to be many paths before us
but all the paths really divide into two.
Which will you take?
The glitter of fool's gold
has been a false light
far too long."

Lifting the Veils

On the afternoon we saw your brother off to America
tired, after weeks of efforting at the embassy
we accidentally locked ourselves out
of your flat in Amarat
and decided to brave the brutal, noon-day sun
for a drink.

I, in my beige dress, the color of sand,
you, in your jacket, the color of the mid-night sky
walked to the only local restaurant, "The Canary"
where foreigners were still permitted to buy
those tall, flat and warm Sudanese beers.

I wondered what the men in white thought
as they served us on the terrace
politely placing the bottle between us
careful not to look into my eyes or address me directly.

We sat for hours sipping the single brew
breaking nearly every taboo
non-muslims, Italian-American, Eritrean,
unmarried lovers,
drinkers of alcohol.
We live dangerously, I thought.

Yet, all that dwarfed and disappeared
when a profound and silent sound echoed from long ago:
Firenze, 13th Century!

The curse of these human eyes,
to see, to sense, but not to clearly prophesize,
to only guess there is a why
to what is more than meets the eye,
to the vision of you and I
meeting in another time,
another forbidden rendezvous of lovers
in the ancient city of Art, Poetry
and that other pair of Great Lovers,
Beatrice and Dante.

Before I could further fix my gaze
this scene had swiftly changed
to a lush garden somewhere in Asia,
where you and I took our final vows of selfless service
before an ancient shrine of Buddha.

Was this a past life memory,
a passage through the barrier of time?
And that afternoon when I vowed
to remain your friend for life,
though I had passionately sought to be your wife
did I know, somewhere deep inside,
that not all of my emotion, devotion or intention
would change a single line
of the pattern that has kept your life
both connected and separated from mine?

Had I come all this way
to discover
the essence of lover and beloved?

Lover of the Gentle Heart

Some will talk, gossip and say
how can you love Him?
You don't even know him.
I say, who is there to know?
I feel a presence and all barriers part.
How can one know what is only space and air?
yet, there is familiarity here
a warm remembrance
a dream within a dream
uninscribed, unlined like an ethereal smile,
a walk I can recognize
in the walks of others,
a path I have traveled
and am yet to embark.
Oh, lover of the gentle heart
you are the Beloved
growing on the insides of my own heart.

Kore

I have known the gnawing at the core
the drive out to fill a gap, an ancient hole
the abyss, empty as a void
and yet... I know what fills this
is neither man nor gold, fame, work or art.

What fills this has no name
yet, wears all names
comes and goes without control,
is more powerful than a million lovers
and The Only Unforgettable One.

Do you know the colors of your soul
its pulsations through the night
that long to make you whole?
Do you know the feelings of the soul
its quiet, peaceful rhythms?
Can you distinguish them from
your ego's hold and its divisions?

When you really listen
can you hear your soul's sweet music,
its inners soundings, a song
or do you give your mind all the power?
Do you know the secrets of the soul,
its longing to reach you
give you all the love that you can hold
treasures untold, greater than gold,
greater than dark or light?

Do you know the soul is found in silence,
has purpose and intention
asks only one question:
Will you open up your heart completely
and willingly sacrifice your pain?

Departure: Beside the Blue Nile

On our last night
June's crescent moon brings
both a celebration and a reflection.

We do the Eritrean snake dance
and appear like a constellation
distinct little stars
in a beautiful configuration.

It feels like a wedding
and for one wondrous moment
I am Krishna among my many lovers.
Love, once having been so narrowly focused
has reopened and expanded
and love's calling, although difficult
has tapped my magical resources.

Excitedly, I wonder
what encounters, starbursts or meteorites
will fly next?
What voids, eternal nights might enter?

The world of high contrast
has taught me
the rivers of pleasure and pain
like woman and man
are in essence the same.

Within each are two currents
which seem to run in opposing streams.
Yet, when we learn their secrets,
we see fire and water blending.

I may never know why this particular desert called me
whether I've lived here before
I know this desert took me
to life's very origins.
Removed from the safe and familiar
I searched more deeply and discovered
that when love calls one
past time, place, gender or race
unto itself, we may find our true essence.

I will come to you again, Mother Nile,
my questions - more cooled and purified.
Next time we will meet in Egypt
where you are One.

The men and I make our final farewells
promising to meet again and to write.
Oh, how quiet is this night...how full.

About the Author

Louisa Calio is an award winning poet and writer. She won First Prize in the IV Concorso Di Poesia Internationale Messina Citta D'Arte, Sicily, November 30, 2013, for her poem "Bhari", in this collection. Louisa was a finalist for Poet Laureate of Nassau County in 2013, Winner of the Connecticut Commission of the Arts Grant to individual writers 1978, the Barbara Jones and Taliesin Prizes for Poetry (Trinidad & Tobago), an ECA arts grant for a multimedia production of her book, In the Eye of Balance, Women in Leadership Award 1987, and honored with Alice Walker, Gloria Steinem, and others as a Feminist Who Changed America (1963-75) at Columbia/ Barnard in 2006. She taught English in Philadelphia and Creative Writing in Connecticut, was Co-founder and first Executive Director of City Spirit Artists, Inc. (1976-1981) a non- profit arts organization in New Haven, Ct. She directed the Poets and Writers Piazza for Hofstra's Italian Experience, 2002-2013, and is on the Advisory Board of Arba Sicula. She completed an exhibition of her photos with poems in "A PASSION FOR AFRICA" and "A PASSION FOR JAMAICA" 1 & 2 at the renowned Round Hill Resort & Villas in Jamaica, West Indies. Her writings appear in numerous anthologies, journals and books.

To learn more go to **Wikipedia: http://en.wikipedia.org/wiki/ Louisa_Calio**

"Louisa Calio's poetry is a veritable chairoscuro of images in black and white, woven together with a profound passion for the lyrical."

*- **Henry Louis Gates, Jr., Renowned Harvard Scholar***

"Louisa Calio is a fresh voice with an exquisite power of translation. Reality becomes spirit, time and again in her verses because she is armed with a formidable translating power based on love."

*- **Robert Farris Thompson, Professor of Art and Religion Yale University***

"Journey to the Heart Waters startles because it is a 20th Century version of the ancient epic of creation, migration and return. An Italian/American woman is drawn by love to travel to the heart waters of Africa where humans emerged, migrated, and where the liberation story of the third millennium is being played out. A brilliant work!

*- **Dr. Lucia Chiavola Birnbaum, International Award Winning Sicilian/ American Author***

"*This is a journey among cultures, America, Italy and Africa, by the extraordinary creative talent of Louisa Calio. She is not just a writer, but a real healer.*"

-Dr. Elisabetta Marino, University of Rome, Tor Vergata

Louisa Calio's "*Journey to the Heart Waters* is a searing personal work of eternal return and transformation. Calio sets out on a quest that unites southern Italy and east Africa through the image and bodies of the Black Madonnas who encourage her to seek, to question, to love, to grieve, to revel and to dance. These poems are a profoundly poignant and well-earned liberation from all that is oppressive in the modern world."

- Dr. Stanislao Pugliese, Hofstra University